Travel *BLOG* Planner *journal*

Kaylee Berry

Weston Tree Publishing

Dedication

To all the adventurous souls.
May you have success in all you write, create,
plan and propose.
I look forward to reading all that comes out of your journal.

Table of Contents

HOW TO USE THIS BOOK

Reader Profile

Use the reader profile to get to know your ideal audience. Fill in every blank to create a complete guide of who your readers are, what they like, and what they want from you.

Writing Tips

Read over the tips in this section often to keep your writing interesting and engaging. It will help you to focus on your readers as you write and therefore create better content.

One Year - One Post a Week Schedule

For most blogs one post a week is enough. Use this one-year planner to come up with a theme for each month. Then plan your posts out for each week. For your convenience 5 weeks are included in case you post on a certain day of the week and there happen to be 5 in a month. You will be able to see a whole years worth of content at a glance.

Post Publishing Checklist

Use this helpful checklist every time you get ready to publish a new post. It has all the steps you need to successfully launch a new post. As a bonus there is an additional checklist of extra ways to create more content using your post.

Journal Pages

Use this journal to collect all your *never-ending* ideas. There is room to write about ways to grow your blog, products to launch, and ideas for posts. If you're ever stuck use the prompts to inspire you. In this section of the book you'll also find a page to record the places you visit, with a sketch box for drawing or adding a photo. You'll also find inspirational quotes to keep you motivated to write, grow your blog, and find success.

Index

Every journal entry has a place to fill in a category. This will allow you to easily categorize your ideas for quick reference later. The index has room for thirteen categories and room enough to write every page number that corresponds with that idea.

IN ORDER TO
HAVE AN AUDIENCE,
YOU MUST WRITE FOR ONE.

-Kaylee Berry

IDEAL READER PROFILE

Name: _____

Age: _____

Location: _____

Occupation: _____

Relationship Status: _____

Religious Preferences: _____

Hobbies: _____

_____

Interests: _____

_____

What are they looking to gain from your blog?_____

_____

_____

What do they spend time online doing? _____

_____

_____

Where do they travel? _____

_____

_____

IDEAL READER PROFILE CONT.

Describe their general disposition and personality: _____

_____

_____

_____

What activities would fill their calendar for the next year? _____

_____

_____

_____

What influences their buying decisions? _____

_____

What would make them trust and respect you? _____

_____

_____

Would they ever spend money on services/products you offer? _____

_____

_____

What would it take for them to purchase them from you? _____

_____

_____

What questions would they ask you if they sat across from you drinking

coffee? _____

_____

_____

_____

_____

THREE QUESTIONS

Ask yourself these questions before you start writing....

Question 1: What am I writing about?

Choose a theme and main topic. Don't try to cram too many things in a single post. Have no more than two sub-points. Otherwise, it will be hard for your readers to follow along.

Question 2: What am I trying to say?

Know which side of the argument you are on. Choose a simple statement that you can easily remember. Write it down next to your workspace and refer to it often. It will be what you base every writing decision on. Think of it as your worldview.

Ex. I believe everyone should experience the wonder of the world.

Ex. Anyone can find money in their budget to travel .

Use your "writers statement" to build all of your content. It will be what you are known for.

Question 3: Who am I writing for?

Imagine your ideal reader every time you form a sentence. Think about how they will receive your words. Try to give them what they want. Entertain them, inspire them, move them to have strong emotions, or whatever your goal is in your writing.

Writing Tips

Put Your Readers First

In order to have an audience, you must write for one. You must think about your reader with every word you write. Picture them receiving your ideas, being entertained by your words, finding inspiration in your stories.

Your audience is your number one priority when you write. Whether you're trying to get your reader to spend some of their hard earned money on your book, trying to teach them something, or sharing your experiences to help others going through a similar situation, you must build trust.

They need to know that you have their best interests at heart. They are looking for someone who is genuine and sharing something that interests them. Your audience wants to be entertained, taught, and inspired. Be the kind of writer that delivers what they want.

Be a Thought Leader

The key to having raving fans is to have killer content. Every word out of your mouth should be prophetic.

Your focus should be on producing something that is life changing to anyone who reads it. Filler and fluff just won't cut it. Use your words to inspire others, and they will inspire others with your words.

When you hear or see something amazing, you want to share it with everyone you know. Your following may start out small, but it will grow over time by people sharing what you say.

It takes more than just experience to be a thought leader. It takes stepping out of the norm and thinking outside of the box. It's a combination of mastery and continual searching. There is still much to be discovered. Be a pioneer. Then report back to everyone the wonderful things you've found.

Show Your Audience You're a Real Person

Let your readers get to know the real you. Tell them stories from your life to help them connect with you. Share your struggles and joys.

Bring your personality to whatever you're writing. Don't hide behind your keyboard and create a persona that doesn't represent you. Use words that you would use in everyday conversation. Slip in a bit of your sense of humor.

Give your readers permission to talk to you directly. In fact, ask them to. At the end of posts or emails, encourage them to respond directly to you. If people like you and get to know you, they will trust you.

Write Like You're Talking to a Friend

Picture yourself dialoguing with your best friend or your ideal reader. Use words and phrases you would use in real conversations. Let the conversation flow from one topic to the next.

When you are with a friend, you're not nervous or self-conscious. You are at ease and feel safe. Your writing should convey those things. Show your readers you are comfortable with them.

Open up to them and let them know your secrets. Create inside jokes that only your readers will understand. You want to build community among the people you write for. They will sense your authenticity and be drawn to you and your work.

Share Your Unique Perspective

You may be thinking to yourself, "There are already a ton of blogs out there. Why would anyone want to read mine?" I personally think there could never be enough blogs. Every writer has their own voice and style that is different from any other. What speaks to one person won't have the same effect on the next. That is why the world needs your voice, to reach others like you.

Whatever interests you, most likely interests other people too. So share your unique perspective, and you will find *your* people. Your distinct approach and knowledge on a specific subject will be unique and put you above the rest.

Make It Interesting

Facts and figures are necessary for some audiences. I understand that, but if you don't make your content interesting and lively readers will pass over your work.

Use things we've talked about like personal stories, your unique take on things, writing like you're talking with a friend, using plain language, adding a bit of your humor.

You can break up text with quote or pictures to make your posts more reader-friendly and break up the large sections of text. Doing this will help to keep your readers attention.

Find Your Voice

Decide how you want to present your information. Are you going to be funny and humorous, sarcastic and snarky, gentle and kind, motherly, edgy? You decide what writing style best fits your personality and include it in every piece you write.

This will be your voice.

Final Thoughts

Writing to influence people can be a big responsibility so always aim to encourage and uplift and don't use your words to tear down.

When you think you've run out of ideas and inspiration for writing, commit to journaling every day. You'll be amazed at the thoughts you have when you give yourself some room to breathe and be creative.

ONE YEAR

ONE POST A

WEEK PLANNER

One Year
One Post a Week Schedule

Month:_____ Theme:_____

Post 1   _____
Post 2   _____
Post 3   _____
Post 4   _____
Post 5   _____

Month:_____ Theme:_____

Post 1   _____
Post 2   _____
Post 3   _____
Post 4   _____
Post 5   _____

Month:_____ Theme:_____

Post 1   _____
Post 2   _____
Post 3   _____
Post 4   _____
Post 5   _____

Month:_____ Theme:_____

Post 1   _____
Post 2   _____
Post 3   _____
Post 4   _____
Post 5   _____

Month _November_   Theme: _Family/Gratitude_
Post 1 _What I'm most thankful for_
Post 2 _10 Ways to Cultivate Gratitude_

Month:_____ Theme:_____

Post 1   _____
Post 2   _____
Post 3   _____
Post 4   _____
Post 5   _____

Month:_____ Theme:_____

Post 1   _____
Post 2   _____
Post 3   _____
Post 4   _____
Post 5   _____

Month:_____ Theme:_____

Post 1   _____
Post 2   _____
Post 3   _____
Post 4   _____
Post 5   _____

Month:_____ Theme:_____

Post 1   _____
Post 2   _____
Post 3   _____
Post 4   _____
Post 5   _____

Month:_____ Theme:_____

Post 1 _____
Post 2 _____
Post 3 _____
Post 4 _____
Post 5 _____

Month:_____ Theme:_____

Post 1 _____
Post 2 _____
Post 3 _____
Post 4 _____
Post 5 _____

Month:_____ Theme:_____

Post 1 _____
Post 2 _____
Post 3 _____
Post 4 _____
Post 5 _____

Month:_____ Theme:_____

Post 1 _____
Post 2 _____
Post 3 _____
Post 4 _____
Post 5 _____

PUBLISHING CHECKLIST & HEADLINE TEMPLATES

Post Publishing Checklist

- ☐ Good Title that builds interest
- ☐ Researched
- ☐ Proofread
- ☐ Grammar Checked
- ☐ Tags added
- ☐ Link to Old Posts
- ☐ Add Feature Image
- ☐ Use Short Paragraphs
- ☐ Break up the text with Images
- ☐ Built in SEO (Search Engine Optimization)
- ☐ Call to Action
- ☐ Pull out quotes
- ☐ Highlight or Bold Important Sections for easy Skimming
- ☐ Share on Social Media Outlets

Create More Content by Re-purposing your Post

- ☐ Create a video
- ☐ Use it for a Podcast
- ☐ Turn it into a series
- ☐ Use it in a book
- ☐ Create a workbook/checklist/template
- ☐ Use the idea to create an E-Course

Blog Post Title/Headline Templates

How to Avoid _____ (bad situation)

Places to Visit Before You Die

What to Pack on a Trip to _____ (destination ex. beach)

Must Have Items for Traveling

Best Practices for Traveling with a Companion

My Best Money Saving Tips for Traveling

The Do's and Don'ts of _____

What Not to-do When You Travel Out of the Country

Best Travel Accessories

How to Find Cheap Travel Destinations

Best Places to Visit in _____

Ultimate Travel Bucket List

Travel-guide to _____

Exploring _____ on a Budget

Best Tips for Travel Photography

Most Beautiful Places I've Ever Visited

Best Packing Tips

What's in My Suitcase? How to pack for _____

Practical Guide to _____

Think you know how to _____

_____

_____

_____

Share

your experiences with this blog planner
on social media.

#TheBlogThatNeverEnds

Title: _____

Category: _____

Date   /   /

What happened to me today that would be interesting/entertaining for my readers?

_____
_____
_____
_____
_____
_____
_____
_____
_____
_____
_____
_____
_____
_____
_____

Notes:_____
_____
_____
_____
_____
_____
_____
_____
_____
_____
_____

☐Drafted   ☐Proofread   ☐Published

Location: _____

_____

Where I Stayed: _____

Places I Visited: _____

_____

My Favorite Part: _____

_____

_____

Advice to anyone wanting to visit: _____

_____

_____

☐Drafted   ☐Proofread   ☐Published   25

Title: _____

Category: _____

What do you look for in a souvenir to give to a friend?

_____
_____
_____
_____
_____
_____
_____
_____
_____
_____
_____
_____
_____
_____

Notes: _____
_____
_____
_____
_____
_____
_____
_____
_____
_____
_____

☐Drafted ☐Proofread ☐Published

Title: _____   Date   /   /

Category: _____

WORDS ARE THE

MEDIUM BY

WHICH WRITERS

CREATE.

-Kaylee Berry

Title: _____

Category: _____

What is something about myself that I've never shared with my readers before?

Notes: _____

☐Drafted   ☐Proofread   ☐Published

Location: _____

_____

Date   /   /

Where I Stayed: _____

Places I Visited: _____

_____

My Favorite Part: _____

_____

_____

Advice to anyone wanting to visit: _____

_____

_____

☐Drafted   ☐Proofread   ☐Published

Title: _____

Category: _____

Date   /   /

What is on my mind today that I can't stop thinking about?

_____
_____
_____
_____
_____
_____
_____
_____
_____
_____
_____
_____
_____
_____
_____

Notes:_____
_____
_____
_____
_____
_____
_____
_____
_____
_____
_____

☐Drafted   ☐Proofread   ☐Published

Title: _____

Category: _____

Date ___ / ___ / ___

> THE WORLD IS
> A BOOK, AND
> THOSE WHO DO
> NOT TRAVEL
> READ ONLY
> A PAGE.
>
> *-Saint Augustine*

Title: _____

Category: _____

Why did I start writing my blog in the first place?

_____

_____

_____

_____

_____

_____

_____

_____

_____

_____

_____

_____

_____

_____

_____

_____

Notes:_____

_____

_____

_____

_____

_____

_____

_____

_____

_____

_____

□Drafted   □Proofread   □Published

Location: _____

_____

Date / /

Where I Stayed: _____

_____

Places I Visited: _____

_____

_____

My Favorite Part: _____

_____

_____

_____

Advice to anyone wanting to visit: _____

_____

_____

_____

Title: _____

Category: _____

Where do you shop to find the best deals on airfare and lodging?

_____
_____
_____
_____
_____
_____
_____
_____
_____
_____
_____
_____
_____
_____
_____

Notes: _____
_____
_____
_____
_____
_____
_____
_____
_____
_____
_____

☐Drafted   ☐Proofread   ☐Published

Title: _____

Category: _____

Date ___ / ___ / ___

> SUCCESS IS NO ACCIDENT. IT IS HARD WORK, PERSEVERANCE, LEARNING, STUDYING, SACRIFICE AND MOST OF ALL, LOVE OF WHAT YOU ARE DOING OR LEARNING TO DO.
>
> *-Pele*

Title: _____

Category: _____

Date   /   /

What are your best tips/hacks for living out of a suitcase?

Notes:_____

☐Drafted   ☐Proofread   ☐Published

Location: _____

_____

Date   /   /

Where I Stayed: _____

_____

Places I Visited: _____

_____

_____

My Favorite Part: _____

_____

_____

_____

Advice to anyone wanting to visit: _____

_____

_____

_____

☐Drafted   ☐Proofread   ☐Published

Title: _____

Category: _____

Date _____ / _____ / _____

What is something new I'd like to try?

Notes: _____

☐Drafted   ☐Proofread   ☐Published

Title: _____

Category: _____

> EITHER WRITE
> SOMETHING
> WORTH
> READING OR
> DO SOMETHING
> WORTH
> WRITING.
>
> -Benjamin Franklin

☐Drafted   ☐Proofread   ☐Published

Title: _____

Category: _____

What does my audience want from me?

_____
_____
_____
_____
_____
_____
_____
_____
_____
_____
_____
_____
_____
_____

Notes: _____
_____
_____
_____
_____
_____
_____
_____
_____
_____

    ☐Drafted   ☐Proofread   ☐Published

Location: _____

_____

Date ___ / ___ / ___

Where I Stayed: _____

_____

Places I Visited: _____

_____

_____

My Favorite Part: _____

_____

_____

_____

Advice to anyone wanting to visit: _____

_____

_____

_____

☐Drafted   ☐Proofread   ☐Published   41

Title: _____

Category: _____

What kinds of souvenirs do I collect for myself?

_____
_____
_____
_____
_____
_____
_____
_____
_____
_____
_____
_____
_____
_____
_____
_____

Notes: _____
_____
_____
_____
_____
_____
_____
_____
_____
_____
_____

☐Drafted   ☐Proofread   ☐Published

Title: _____

Category: _____

Date ___ / ___ / ___

> I DO NOT SEE THE
> PROCESS OF BLOGGING
> AS A SEPARATE THING
> FROM CREATING ART.
> THIS IS IN PART WHY
> I DO NOT LIKE TO BE
> KNOWN FOR BEING
> A 'BLOGGER,' AS THIS
> IS JUST ONE FORM OF
> OUTPUT FOR CREATIVE
> IDEAS.
>
> *-Keri Smith*

☐Drafted   ☐Proofread   ☐Published

Title: _____

Category: _____

Do you ever stop and ask the locals for advice on places to visit?

_____
_____
_____
_____
_____
_____
_____
_____
_____
_____
_____
_____
_____
_____
_____
_____

Notes: _____
_____
_____
_____
_____
_____
_____
_____
_____
_____
_____
_____

☐Drafted   ☐Proofread   ☐Published

Location: _____

_____

Date ___ / ___ / ___

Where I Stayed: _____

_____

Places I Visited: _____

_____

_____

My Favorite Part: _____

_____

_____

_____

Advice to anyone wanting to visit: _____

_____

_____

_____

☐Drafted   ☐Proofread   ☐Published   45

Title: _____

Category: _____

Who is my favorite blogger and why?

_____
_____
_____
_____
_____
_____
_____
_____
_____
_____
_____
_____
_____
_____

Notes: _____
_____
_____
_____
_____
_____
_____
_____
_____
_____

☐Drafted   ☐Proofread   ☐Published

Title: _____

Category: _____

Date ___/___/___

TRAVELING.
IT LEAVES YOU
SPEECHLESS,
THEN TURNS
YOU INTO A
STORYTELLER.

- *Ibn Battuta*

☐Drafted   ☐Proofread   ☐Published   47

Title: _____

Category: _____

What do your refuse to travel without?

_____
_____
_____
_____
_____
_____
_____
_____
_____
_____
_____
_____
_____
_____
_____
_____

Notes:_____
_____
_____
_____
_____
_____
_____
_____
_____
_____
_____
_____

☐Drafted   ☐Proofread   ☐Published

Location: _____

_____

Date   /   /

Where I Stayed: _____

Places I Visited: _____

_____

_____

My Favorite Part: _____

_____

_____

_____

Advice to anyone wanting to visit: _____

_____

_____

_____

Title: _____

Category: _____

Who do you like to travel with?

_____
_____
_____
_____
_____
_____
_____
_____
_____
_____
_____
_____
_____
_____
_____
_____

Notes:_____
_____
_____
_____
_____
_____
_____
_____
_____
_____
_____

☐Drafted   ☐Proofread   ☐Published

Title: _____

Category: _____

Date   /   /

LIFE IS EITHER
A GREAT
ADVENTURE OR
NOTHING.

-Helen Keller

Title: _____

Category: _____

What is my favorite part of being a blogger?

Notes: _____

☐Drafted   ☐Proofread   ☐Published

Location: _____

_____

Date ____ / ____ / ____

Where I Stayed: _____

_____

Places I Visited: _____

_____

_____

My Favorite Part: _____

_____

_____

Advice to anyone wanting to visit: _____

_____

_____

_____

☐Drafted   ☐Proofread   ☐Published   53

Title: _____

Category: _____

Date   /   /

What area of blogging do I struggle with most?

_____
_____
_____
_____
_____
_____
_____
_____
_____
_____
_____
_____
_____

Notes:_____
_____
_____
_____
_____
_____
_____
_____
_____
_____

☐Drafted   ☐Proofread   ☐Published

Title: _____

Category: _____

Date   /   /

> EVERY DAY IS A
> JOURNEY, AND
> THE JOURNEY
> ITSELF IS HOME.
>
> -Matsuo Basho

Title: _____

Category: _____

What advice would I give to my younger self?

_____
_____
_____
_____
_____
_____
_____
_____
_____
_____
_____
_____
_____
_____
_____
_____

Notes:_____
_____
_____
_____
_____
_____
_____
_____
_____
_____
_____

☐Drafted   ☐Proofread   ☐Published

Location: _____

_____

Where I Stayed: _____

_____

Places I Visited: _____

_____

_____

My Favorite Part: _____

_____

_____

_____

Advice to anyone wanting to visit: _____

_____

_____

_____

☐Drafted   ☐Proofread   ☐Published

Title: _____

Category: _____

What have I read recently that inspired me?

_____
_____
_____
_____
_____
_____
_____
_____
_____
_____
_____
_____
_____
_____
_____

Notes:_____
_____
_____
_____
_____
_____
_____
_____
_____
_____
_____

☐Drafted   ☐Proofread   ☐Published

Title: _____

Category: _____

Date   /   /

ADVENTURE IS

WORTHWHILE

IN ITSELF.

-Amelia Earhart

Title: _____

Category: _____

Date   /   /

Do you use travel guides when planning a trip? Which ones are your favorite?

_____
_____
_____
_____
_____
_____
_____
_____
_____
_____
_____
_____
_____
_____
_____
_____

Notes:_____
_____
_____
_____
_____
_____
_____
_____
_____
_____
_____
_____

☐Drafted   ☐Proofread   ☐Published

Location: _____

_____

Date _____ / _____ / _____

My Favorite Part: _____

_____

_____

_____

Where I Stayed: _____

_____

Places I Visited: _____

_____

_____

My Favorite Part: _____

_____

_____

_____

Advice to anyone wanting to visit: _____

_____

_____

_____

Title: _____

Category: _____

Date   /   /

What could I teach my audience?

_____
_____
_____
_____
_____
_____
_____
_____
_____
_____
_____
_____
_____
_____
_____

Notes: _____
_____
_____
_____
_____
_____
_____
_____
_____
_____
_____

     ☐Drafted   ☐Proofread   ☐Published

Title: _____

Category: _____

Date ___ / ___ / ___

> SOME PEOPLE
> DREAM OF
> SUCCESS, WHILE
> OTHER PEOPLE
> GET UP EVERY
> MORNING
> AND MAKE IT
> HAPPEN.
>
> *-Wayne Huizenga*

Title: _____

Category: _____

What is my biggest struggle in life?

_____
_____
_____
_____
_____
_____
_____
_____
_____
_____
_____
_____
_____
_____
_____

Notes: _____
_____
_____
_____
_____
_____
_____
_____
_____
_____
_____
_____

☐Drafted ☐Proofread ☐Published

Location: _____

_____

Date   /   /

Where I Stayed: _____

_____

Places I Visited: _____

_____

_____

My Favorite Part: _____

_____

_____

Advice to anyone wanting to visit: _____

_____

_____

_____

☐Drafted   ☐Proofread   ☐Published

Title: _____

Category: _____

If someone was coming to visit your hometown, what would you recommend them to see/do?

_____
_____
_____
_____
_____
_____
_____
_____
_____
_____
_____
_____
_____
_____
_____
_____

Notes: _____
_____
_____
_____
_____
_____
_____
_____
_____
_____
_____
_____

☐Drafted   ☐Proofread   ☐Published

Title: _____

Category: _____

> HABITS LIKE
> BLOGGING OFTEN AND
> REGULARLY, WRITING
> DOWN THE WAY YOU
> THINK, BEING CLEAR
> ABOUT WHAT YOU
> THINK ARE EFFECTIVE
> TACTICS, IGNORING
> THE BURBLING CROWD
> ...ALL OF THESE ARE
> USEFUL HABITS.
>
> *-Seth Godin*

☐Drafted   ☐Proofread   ☐Published

Title: _____

Category: _____

Date   /   /

What marketing ideas do I have for my blog?

_____
_____
_____
_____
_____
_____
_____
_____
_____
_____
_____
_____
_____
_____

Notes:_____
_____
_____
_____
_____
_____
_____
_____
_____
_____
_____

☐Drafted   ☐Proofread   ☐Published

Location: _____

_____

Date ___ / ___ / ___

Where I Stayed: _____

_____

Places I Visited: _____

_____

_____

My Favorite Part:_____

_____

_____

_____

Advice to anyone wanting to visit: _____

_____

_____

_____

☐Drafted   ☐Proofread   ☐Published   69

Title: _____

Date   /   /

Category: _____

What traits do you look for in a traveling partner?

_____
_____
_____
_____
_____
_____
_____
_____
_____
_____
_____
_____
_____
_____
_____

Notes: _____
_____
_____
_____
_____
_____
_____
_____
_____
_____
_____

☐Drafted   ☐Proofread   ☐Published

Title: _____

Category: _____

Date ___ / ___ / ___

> THOUGH WE
> TRAVEL THE WORLD
> OVER TO FIND
> THE BEAUTIFUL,
> WE MUST CARRY
> IT WITH US OR WE
> FIND IT NOT.
>
> *-Ralph Waldo Emerson*

Title: _____

Category: _____

Date   /   /

If I were to start another blog what would it be about?

_____
_____
_____
_____
_____
_____
_____
_____
_____
_____
_____
_____
_____
_____

Notes:_____
_____
_____
_____
_____
_____
_____
_____
_____
_____
_____

☐Drafted   ☐Proofread   ☐Published

Location: _____

_____

Date ____ / ____ / ____

☀ ⛅ ☁ 🌧 ⛈ ⛈

My Favorite Part: _____

Where I Stayed: _____
_____

Places I Visited: _____
_____
_____

My Favorite Part: _____
_____
_____
_____

Advice to anyone wanting to visit: _____
_____
_____
_____

Title: _____

Category: _____

Date   /   /

Where is the scariest place I've ever stayed while traveling?

_____
_____
_____
_____
_____
_____
_____
_____
_____
_____
_____
_____
_____
_____
_____

Notes:_____
_____
_____
_____
_____
_____
_____
_____
_____
_____
_____

☐Drafted   ☐Proofread   ☐Published

Title: _____

Category: _____

YOUR WRITING VOICE
IS THE DEEPEST
POSSIBLE REFLECTION
OF WHO YOU ARE....
IN YOUR VOICE, YOUR
READERS SHOULD BE
ABLE TO HEAR THE
CONTENTS OF YOUR
MIND, YOUR HEART,
YOUR SOUL.

-Meg Rosoff

☐Drafted   ☐Proofread   ☐Published

Title: _____

Category: _____

Date   /   /

What is your best advice for planning a trip?

_____
_____
_____
_____
_____
_____
_____
_____
_____
_____
_____
_____
_____
_____
_____
_____

Notes:_____
_____
_____
_____
_____
_____
_____
_____
_____
_____
_____
_____

☐Drafted   ☐Proofread   ☐Published

Location: _____

_____

Date   /   /

Where I Stayed: _____
_____

Places I Visited: _____
_____
_____

My Favorite Part: _____
_____
_____
_____

Advice to anyone wanting to visit: _____
_____
_____
_____

Title: _____

Category:_____

Write up a proposal to publish a guest post on your favorite blog?

_____
_____
_____
_____
_____
_____
_____
_____
_____
_____
_____
_____
_____
_____

Notes:_____
_____
_____
_____
_____
_____
_____
_____
_____
_____
_____
_____

☐Drafted   ☐Proofread   ☐Published

Title: _____

Category: _____

WHEREVER
YOU GO, GO
WITH ALL YOUR
HEART.

-Confucius

☐Drafted   ☐Proofread   ☐Published

Title: _____

Date   /   /

Category: _____

Do you enjoy flying? Why or why not?

_____
_____
_____
_____
_____
_____
_____
_____
_____
_____
_____
_____
_____
_____

Notes: _____
_____
_____
_____
_____
_____
_____
_____
_____
_____
_____

☐Drafted ☐Proofread ☐Published

Location: _____

_____

Date _____ / _____ / _____

Where I Stayed: _____

_____

Places I Visited: _____

_____

_____

My Favorite Part: _____

_____

_____

_____

Advice to anyone wanting to visit: _____

_____

_____

_____

☐Drafted   ☐Proofread   ☐Published

Title: _____

Category: _____

What is your best tips for someone who has never flown on a plane?

_____
_____
_____
_____
_____
_____
_____
_____
_____
_____
_____
_____
_____
_____
_____

Notes: _____
_____
_____
_____
_____
_____
_____
_____
_____
_____
_____
_____

☐Drafted   ☐Proofread   ☐Published

Title: _____

Category: _____

> HAPPINESS LIES IN THE JOY OF ACHIEVEMENT AND THE THRILL OF CREATIVE EFFORT.
>
> *-Franklin D. Roosevelt*

Title: _____

Date   /   /

Category: _____

If you could only take 10 items with you on a cruise, what would they be?

_____
_____
_____
_____
_____
_____
_____
_____
_____
_____
_____
_____
_____
_____
_____
_____

Notes:_____
_____
_____
_____
_____
_____
_____
_____
_____
_____
_____
_____
_____

☐Drafted   ☐Proofread   ☐Published

Location: _____

_____

Where I Stayed: _____

_____

Places I Visited: _____

_____

_____

My Favorite Part:_____

_____

_____

_____

Advice to anyone wanting to visit: _____

_____

_____

_____

☐Drafted   ☐Proofread   ☐Published   85

Title: _____

Category: _____

Have you visited a third-world county? Describe your experience or why you'd like to visit in the future.

Notes: _____

☐Drafted   ☐Proofread   ☐Published

Title: _____

Category: _____

Date _____ / _____ / _____

> TO TRAVEL IS TO
>
> TAKE A JOURNEY
>
> INTO YOURSELF.
>
> *-Danny Kaye*

Title: _____

Category:_____

Tell your readers about your day? Do you have a routine you follow?

_____
_____
_____
_____
_____
_____
_____
_____
_____
_____
_____
_____
_____
_____

Notes:_____
_____
_____
_____
_____
_____
_____
_____
_____
_____
_____
_____

☐Drafted   ☐Proofread   ☐Published

Location: _____

_____

Where I Stayed: _____

Places I Visited: _____

_____

My Favorite Part:_____

_____

_____

Advice to anyone wanting to visit: _____

_____

_____

_____

☐Drafted   ☐Proofread   ☐Published   89

Title: _____

Category: _____

Date   /   /

Visualize your blog being a success. What does that look like to you?

_____
_____
_____
_____
_____
_____
_____
_____
_____
_____
_____
_____
_____
_____
_____

Notes:_____
_____
_____
_____
_____
_____
_____
_____
_____
_____
_____

☐Drafted   ☐Proofread   ☐Published

Title: _____

Category: _____

Date   /   /

A MILLION AND
ONE THOUGHTS
FLY THROUGH MY
BRAIN EVERY DAY.
IF I DON'T WRITE
SOME OF THEM
DOWN BRILLIANT
IDEAS COULD BE
LOST.

-Kaylee Berry

Title: _____

Category: _____

Have you ever been to a place where you didn't speak the language?
Describe the experience.

_____

_____

_____

_____

_____

_____

_____

_____

_____

_____

_____

_____

_____

_____

_____

_____

Notes:_____

_____

_____

_____

_____

_____

_____

_____

_____

_____

☐Drafted   ☐Proofread   ☐Published

Location: _____

_____

<table>
<tr><td>Date   /   /</td></tr>
</table>

Where I Stayed: _____

_____

Places I Visited: _____

_____

_____

My Favorite Part: _____

_____

_____

_____

Advice to anyone wanting to visit: _____

_____

_____

_____

☐Drafted   ☐Proofread   ☐Published

Title: _____   Date   /   /

Category: _____

Have you ever taken a long train ride? How did you pass the time?

_____

_____

_____

_____

_____

_____

_____

_____

_____

_____

_____

_____

_____

_____

Notes:_____

_____

_____

_____

_____

_____

_____

_____

_____

_____

☐Drafted   ☐Proofread   ☐Published

Title: _____

Category: _____

Date   /   /

BE BRAVE. TAKE
RISKS. NOTHING
CAN SUBSTITUTE
EXPERIENCE.

-Paulo Coelho

Title: _____

Category: _____

What would I like to do a series of blog posts on?

_____
_____
_____
_____
_____
_____
_____
_____
_____
_____
_____
_____
_____
_____

Notes: _____
_____
_____
_____
_____
_____
_____
_____
_____
_____
_____

☐Drafted ☐Proofread ☐Published

Location: _____

_____

Date   /   /

Where I Stayed: _____

Places I Visited: _____

_____

_____

My Favorite Part: _____

_____

_____

_____

Advice to anyone wanting to visit: _____

_____

_____

_____

☐Drafted   ☐Proofread   ☐Published   97

Title: _____

Category: _____

Date   /   /

What is something I would like to do, but feel like it's out of my comfort zone?

_____
_____
_____
_____
_____
_____
_____
_____
_____
_____
_____
_____
_____

Notes:_____
_____
_____
_____
_____
_____
_____
_____
_____
_____
_____

□Drafted   □Proofread   □Published

Title: _____

Category: _____

Date   /   /

THESE DAYS, YOU
HAVE THE OPTION
OF STAYING HOME,
BLOGGING IN YOUR
UNDERWEAR, AND
NOT HAVING YOUR
WORDS MANGLED.
I THINK I LIKE THE
DIRECTION THINGS
ARE HEADED.

-Marc Andreessen

Title: _____

Category: _____

Where is your favorite place to visit?

_____
_____
_____
_____
_____
_____
_____
_____
_____
_____
_____
_____
_____
_____

Notes: _____
_____
_____
_____
_____
_____
_____
_____
_____
_____
_____

☐Drafted   ☐Proofread   ☐Published

Location: _____

_____

Where I Stayed: _____

_____

Places I Visited: _____

_____

_____

My Favorite Part: _____

_____

_____

_____

Advice to anyone wanting to visit: _____

_____

_____

_____

☐Drafted   ☐Proofread   ☐Published   101

Title: _____

Category: _____

How can I grow my email list this month?

_____
_____
_____
_____
_____
_____
_____
_____
_____
_____
_____
_____
_____
_____
_____

Notes:_____
_____
_____
_____
_____
_____
_____
_____
_____
_____
_____
_____

☐Drafted   ☐Proofread   ☐Published

Title: _____

Category: _____

SUCCESS IS
NOT THE KEY
TO HAPPINESS.
HAPPINESS IS THE
KEY TO SUCCESS. IF
YOU LOVE WHAT
YOU ARE DOING,
YOU WILL BE
SUCCESSFUL.

-Albert Schweitzer

☐Drafted   ☐Proofread   ☐Published

Title: _____

Category: _____

What kind of giveaway/freebie could I create to go with my most popular post?

_____
_____
_____
_____
_____
_____
_____
_____
_____
_____
_____
_____
_____

Notes: _____
_____
_____
_____
_____
_____
_____
_____
_____
_____
_____

☐Drafted   ☐Proofread   ☐Published

Location: _____

_____

Where I Stayed: _____

_____

Places I Visited: _____

_____

_____

My Favorite Part: _____

_____

_____

_____

Advice to anyone wanting to visit: _____

_____

_____

_____

☐Drafted   ☐Proofread   ☐Published

Title: _____

Category: _____

Is there any affiliate programs I need to check out? List them below.

_____

_____

_____

_____

_____

_____

_____

_____

_____

_____

_____

_____

_____

_____

Notes:_____

_____

_____

_____

_____

_____

_____

_____

_____

_____

    ☐Drafted   ☐Proofread   ☐Published

Title: _____

Category: _____

A GOOD
TRAVELER HAS NO
FIXED PLANS, AND
IS NOT INTENT ON
ARRIVING.

-Lao Tzu

Title: _____

Category: _____

What product or service am I loving right now that I could write a review about?

_____
_____
_____
_____
_____
_____
_____
_____
_____
_____
_____
_____
_____
_____

Notes:_____
_____
_____
_____
_____
_____
_____
_____
_____
_____

☐Drafted   ☐Proofread   ☐Published

Location: _____

_____

Date ___ / ___ / ___

Where I Stayed: _____

Places I Visited: _____

My Favorite Part: _____

Advice to anyone wanting to visit: _____

☐Drafted   ☐Proofread   ☐Published

Title: _____

Category: _____

Have you ever asked "Are we there yet"?

_____
_____
_____
_____
_____
_____
_____
_____
_____
_____
_____
_____
_____
_____

Notes: _____
_____
_____
_____
_____
_____
_____
_____
_____
_____
_____
_____

☐Drafted   ☐Proofread   ☐Published

Title: _____

Category: _____

Date   /   /

> WRITING MEANS
> SHARING. IT'S PART
> OF THE HUMAN
> CONDITION
> TO WANT TO
> SHARE THINGS -
> THOUGHTS, IDEAS,
> OPINIONS.
>
> *-Paulo Coelho*

Title: _____

Category: _____

What am I thankful for today?

_____
_____
_____
_____
_____
_____
_____
_____
_____
_____
_____
_____
_____
_____

Notes:_____
_____
_____
_____
_____
_____
_____
_____
_____
_____
_____

☐Drafted   ☐Proofread   ☐Published

Location: _____

_____

Date ____ / ____ / ____

Where I Stayed: _____

_____

Places I Visited: _____

_____

_____

My Favorite Part: _____

_____

_____

_____

Advice to anyone wanting to visit: _____

_____

_____

_____

☐Drafted   ☐Proofread   ☐Published

Title: _____

Date ___ / ___ / ___

Category: _____

How can I improve my writing productivity?

Notes: _____

☐Drafted   ☐Proofread   ☐Published

Title: _____

Category: _____

Date   /   /

THE SECRET OF
YOUR SUCCESS
IS DETERMINED
BY YOUR DAILY
AGENDA.

-John C. Maxwell

Title: _____

Date   /   /

Category: _____

What is my blogs story?

_____
_____
_____
_____
_____
_____
_____
_____
_____
_____
_____
_____
_____
_____
_____

Notes: _____
_____
_____
_____
_____
_____
_____
_____
_____
_____
_____
_____

    ☐Drafted   ☐Proofread   ☐Published

Location: _____

_____

Date   /   /

Where I Stayed: _____

_____

Places I Visited: _____

_____

_____

My Favorite Part: _____

_____

_____

_____

Advice to anyone wanting to visit: _____

_____

_____

_____

☐Drafted   ☐Proofread   ☐Published

Title: _____

Category: _____

Pretend you are going to the beach for the weekend. What do you pack?

_____
_____
_____
_____
_____
_____
_____
_____
_____
_____
_____
_____
_____

Notes:_____
_____
_____
_____
_____
_____
_____
_____
_____
_____
_____

    ☐Drafted   ☐Proofread   ☐Published

Title: _____

Category: _____

Date   /   /

THE BEST
EDUCATION
I HAVE EVER
RECEIVED WAS
THROUGH
TRAVEL.

-Lisa Ling

☐Drafted   ☐Proofread   ☐Published

Title: _____

Category: _____

Do you play games in the car to pass the time while traveling?
What's your favorite?

_____
_____
_____
_____
_____
_____
_____
_____
_____
_____
_____
_____
_____
_____

Notes: _____
_____
_____
_____
_____
_____
_____
_____
_____
_____

☐Drafted   ☐Proofread   ☐Published

Location: _____

_____

Date ___ / ___ / ___

Where I Stayed: _____

Places I Visited: _____

_____

_____

My Favorite Part: _____

_____

_____

_____

Advice to anyone wanting to visit: _____

_____

_____

_____

☐Drafted   ☐Proofread   ☐Published   121

Title: _____

Date   /   /

Category:_____

What are your best tips for traveling on a budget?

_____
_____
_____
_____
_____
_____
_____
_____
_____
_____
_____
_____
_____
_____

Notes:_____
_____
_____
_____
_____
_____
_____
_____
_____
_____
_____

☐Drafted   ☐Proofread   ☐Published

Title: _____

Category: _____

Date   /   /

I SEE MY PATH, BUT
I DON'T KNOW
WHERE IT LEADS.
NOT KNOWING
WHERE I'M GOING
IS WHAT INSPIRES
ME TO TRAVEL IT.

-Rosalia de Castro

☐Drafted   ☐Proofread   ☐Published

Title: _____   Date   /   /

Category: _____

What is my favorite post I've written to date? Could I do a follow up post?

_____
_____
_____
_____
_____
_____
_____
_____
_____
_____
_____
_____
_____

Notes:_____
_____
_____
_____
_____
_____
_____
_____
_____
_____

☐Drafted   ☐Proofread   ☐Published

Location: _____

_____

Date _____ / _____ / _____

☀ ⛅ ☁ 🌧 🌧 ⛈

[ ]

Where I Stayed: _____

Places I Visited: _____

_____

My Favorite Part: _____

_____

_____

Advice to anyone wanting to visit: _____

_____

_____

_____

Title: _____

Date   /   /

Category: _____

What is the best advice I ever got?

_____
_____
_____
_____
_____
_____
_____
_____
_____
_____
_____
_____
_____
_____

Notes: _____
_____
_____
_____
_____
_____
_____
_____
_____
_____
_____

☐Drafted   ☐Proofread   ☐Published

Title: _____

Category: _____

Date ___ / ___ / ___

> BE PATIENT,
> WORK HARD AND
> CONSISTENTLY,
> HAVE FAITH IN
> YOUR WRITING,
> AND DON'T BE
> AFRAID TO LISTEN
> TO CONSTRUCTIVE
> CRITICISM.
>
> *-Jonathan Galassi*

☐ Drafted   ☐ Proofread   ☐ Published

Title: _____

Category: _____

Why do I love traveling?

_____

_____

_____

_____

_____

_____

_____

_____

_____

_____

_____

_____

_____

_____

Notes: _____

_____

_____

_____

_____

_____

_____

_____

_____

_____

_____

☐Drafted   ☐Proofread   ☐Published

Location: _____

_____

Date   /   /

Where I Stayed: _____

_____

Places I Visited: _____

_____

_____

My Favorite Part: _____

_____

_____

_____

Advice to anyone wanting to visit: _____

_____

_____

_____

☐Drafted   ☐Proofread   ☐Published   129

Title: _____

Date   /   /

Category: _____

What creative way can I market my blog this week?

_____
_____
_____
_____
_____
_____
_____
_____
_____
_____
_____
_____
_____
_____

Notes:_____
_____
_____
_____
_____
_____
_____
_____
_____
_____
_____

☐Drafted   ☐Proofread   ☐Published

Title: _____

Category: _____

Date   /   /

THE STARTING
POINT OF ALL
ACHIEVEMENT IS
DESIRE.

-Napoleon Hill

☐Drafted   ☐Proofread   ☐Published

Title: _____   Date   /   /

Category: _____

What inspired me today?

_____
_____
_____
_____
_____
_____
_____
_____
_____
_____
_____
_____
_____
_____
_____

Notes:_____
_____
_____
_____
_____
_____
_____
_____
_____
_____
_____

☐Drafted   ☐Proofread   ☐Published

Location: _____

_____

Where I Stayed: _____

Places I Visited: _____

_____

My Favorite Part: _____

_____

_____

Advice to anyone wanting to visit: _____

_____

_____

_____

☐Drafted   ☐Proofread   ☐Published   133

Title: _____

Category: _____

Did you travel a lot while you were a child?

_____
_____
_____
_____
_____
_____
_____
_____
_____
_____
_____
_____
_____
_____

Notes: _____
_____
_____
_____
_____
_____
_____
_____
_____
_____
_____

□Drafted   □Proofread   □Published

Title: _____

Category: _____

TRAVEL BECOMES

A STRATEGY FOR

ACCUMULATING

PHOTOGRAPHS.

-Susan Sontag

Title: _____

Category: _____

What is one place you would never visit again and why?

_____
_____
_____
_____
_____
_____
_____
_____
_____
_____
_____
_____
_____
_____
_____

Notes: _____
_____
_____
_____
_____
_____
_____
_____
_____
_____
_____
_____

☐Drafted   ☐Proofread   ☐Published

Location: _____

_____

Date ___ / ___ / ___

Where I Stayed: _____

_____

Places I Visited: _____

_____

_____

My Favorite Part:_____

_____

_____

_____

Advice to anyone wanting to visit: _____

_____

_____

_____

Title: _____   Date   /   /

Category: _____

If I could do anything, knowing I wouldn't fail, What would I do?

_____
_____
_____
_____
_____
_____
_____
_____
_____
_____
_____
_____

Notes:_____
_____
_____
_____
_____
_____
_____
_____
_____
_____

☐Drafted   ☐Proofread   ☐Published

Title: _____

Category: _____

> I MADE A DECISION TO WRITE FOR MY READERS, NOT TO TRY TO FIND MORE READERS FOR MY WRITING.
>
> *-Seth Godin*

☐Drafted   ☐Proofread   ☐Published

Title: _____   Date   /   /

Category: _____

What unique experiences have I had in my life that I can share with my audience?

Notes: _____

☐Drafted   ☐Proofread   ☐Published

Location: _____

_____

Where I Stayed: _____

_____

Places I Visited: _____

_____

_____

My Favorite Part: _____

_____

_____

_____

Advice to anyone wanting to visit: _____

_____

_____

_____

☐Drafted   ☐Proofread   ☐Published

Title: _____   Date   /   /

Category: _____

Are you easy to travel with? Be honest

_____
_____
_____
_____
_____
_____
_____
_____
_____
_____
_____
_____
_____
_____
_____

Notes:_____
_____
_____
_____
_____
_____
_____
_____
_____
_____
_____
_____

☐Drafted   ☐Proofread   ☐Published

Title: _____

Category: _____

> THE TRAVELER
> SEES WHAT HE
> SEES, THE TOURIST
> SEES WHAT HE HAS
> COME TO SEE.
>
> -*Gilbert K. Chesterton*

☐Drafted   ☐Proofread   ☐Published

Title: _____ Date   /   /

Category: _____

What is one life lesson I had to learn the hard way?

_____
_____
_____
_____
_____
_____
_____
_____
_____
_____
_____
_____
_____

Notes: _____
_____
_____
_____
_____
_____
_____
_____
_____
_____
_____

☐Drafted ☐Proofread ☐Published

Location: _____

_____

Date   /   /

Where I Stayed: _____

_____

Places I Visited: _____

_____

_____

My Favorite Part: _____

_____

_____

Advice to anyone wanting to visit: _____

_____

_____

_____

☐Drafted   ☐Proofread   ☐Published

Title: _____   Date   /   /

Category: _____

What is your favorite part about visiting a new place?

Notes: _____

☐Drafted   ☐Proofread   ☐Published

Title: _____

Category: _____

> THE DISCIPLINE
> OF WRITING
> SOMETHING
> DOWN IS THE
> FIRST STEP
> TOWARD MAKING
> IT HAPPEN.
>
> *-Lee Iacocca*

☐Drafted   ☐Proofread   ☐Published

Title: _____

Category: _____

Is there a certain type of store/establishment you visit in every place you travel? Ex. bakery, antique store

_____
_____
_____
_____
_____
_____
_____
_____
_____
_____
_____
_____
_____
_____
_____

Notes:_____
_____
_____
_____
_____
_____
_____
_____
_____
_____
_____
_____

☐Drafted   ☐Proofread   ☐Published

Location: _____

_____

Date   /   /

Where I Stayed: _____

_____

Places I Visited: _____

_____

_____

My Favorite Part: _____

_____

_____

_____

Advice to anyone wanting to visit: _____

_____

_____

_____

☐Drafted   ☐Proofread   ☐Published   149

Title: _____

Category: _____

What is one place you have visited before and would love to visit again?

_____

_____

_____

_____

_____

_____

_____

_____

_____

_____

_____

_____

_____

_____

Notes: _____

_____

_____

_____

_____

_____

_____

_____

_____

_____

_____

_____

☐Drafted   ☐Proofread   ☐Published

Title: _____

Category: _____

NEVER GO ON

TRIPS WITH

ANYONE YOU DO

NOT LOVE.

-Ernest Hemingway

☐Drafted   ☐Proofread   ☐Published

Title: _____

Category: _____

In what ways can I give back to my community, either online or in person?

_____

_____

_____

_____

_____

_____

_____

_____

_____

_____

_____

_____

_____

_____

Notes:_____

_____

_____

_____

_____

_____

_____

_____

_____

_____

_____

☐Drafted   ☐Proofread   ☐Published

Location: _____

_____

Date ___ / ___ / ___

Where I Stayed: _____

_____

Places I Visited: _____

_____

_____

My Favorite Part: _____

_____

_____

_____

Advice to anyone wanting to visit: _____

_____

_____

_____

Title: _____

Category: _____

Brainstorm ideas for holiday posts?

Notes: _____

☐Drafted   ☐Proofread   ☐Published

Title: _____

Category: _____

Date   /   /

> ALL JOURNEYS
> HAVE SECRET
> DESTINATIONS
> OF WHICH THE
> TRAVELER IS
> UNAWARE.
> -*Martin Buber*

Title: _____

Date   /   /

Category: _____

Where are you planning your next trip?

_____
_____
_____
_____
_____
_____
_____
_____
_____
_____
_____
_____
_____
_____
_____
_____

Notes:_____
_____
_____
_____
_____
_____
_____
_____
_____
_____
_____
_____
_____

☐Drafted   ☐Proofread   ☐Published

Location: _____

_____

Where I Stayed: _____

_____

Places I Visited: _____

_____

_____

My Favorite Part: _____

_____

_____

_____

Advice to anyone wanting to visit: _____

_____

_____

_____

☐Drafted   ☐Proofread   ☐Published   157

Title: _____

Date   /   /

Category:_____

What is your favorite way to travel? Ex. car, plane, bus

Notes:_____

     ☐Drafted   ☐Proofread   ☐Published

Title: _____

Category: _____

> EXPLORATION
> IS REALLY THE
> ESSENCE OF THE
> HUMAN SPIRIT.
>
> *-Frank Borman*

☐Drafted   ☐Proofread   ☐Published

Title: _____

Category: _____

Date   /   /

Do you keep a travel diary? Share your favorite entry or start one today.

_____
_____
_____
_____
_____
_____
_____
_____
_____
_____
_____
_____
_____
_____

Notes: _____
_____
_____
_____
_____
_____
_____
_____
_____
_____
_____

☐Drafted ☐Proofread ☐Published

Location: _____

_____

Where I Stayed: _____

Places I Visited: _____

_____

_____

My Favorite Part: _____

_____

_____

_____

Advice to anyone wanting to visit: _____

_____

_____

_____

☐Drafted   ☐Proofread   ☐Published

Title: _____

Category: _____

Date   /   /

How will I attract new readers to my blog?

_____
_____
_____
_____
_____
_____
_____
_____
_____
_____
_____
_____
_____
_____

Notes:_____
_____
_____
_____
_____
_____
_____
_____
_____
_____
_____
_____
_____

☐Drafted   ☐Proofread   ☐Published

Title: _____

Category: _____

THE SECRET OF
GOOD WRITING
IS TO SAY AN OLD
THING IN A NEW
WAY OR TO SAY A
NEW THING IN AN
OLD WAY.

-Richard Harding Davis

☐Drafted   ☐Proofread   ☐Published

Title: _____

Category:_____

If someone surprises you with a vacation, and you have no idea where you are going, what do you pack?

Notes:_____

☐Drafted   ☐Proofread   ☐Published

Location: _____

_____

Where I Stayed: _____

_____

Places I Visited: _____

_____

_____

My Favorite Part: _____

_____

_____

_____

Advice to anyone wanting to visit: _____

_____

_____

_____

☐Drafted   ☐Proofread   ☐Published

Title: _____

Date / /

Category: _____

Write a list of thoughtful souvenirs to give to loved ones?

_____
_____
_____
_____
_____
_____
_____
_____
_____
_____
_____
_____
_____
_____

Notes:_____
_____
_____
_____
_____
_____
_____
_____
_____
_____
_____

☐Drafted ☐Proofread ☐Published

Title: _____

Category: _____

> COMMUNICATION
> - THE HUMAN
> CONNECTION -
> IS THE KEY TO
> PERSONAL AND
> CAREER SUCCESS.
>
> -Paul J. Meyer

Product Reviews

☆☆☆☆☆

Product Name: _____

Company: _____

Thoughts: _____

_____

_____

_____

☆☆☆☆☆

Product Name: _____

Company: _____

Thoughts: _____

_____

_____

_____

☆☆☆☆☆

Product Name: _____

Company: _____

Thoughts: _____

_____

_____

_____

☆☆☆☆☆

Product Name: _____

Company: _____

Thoughts: _____

_____

_____

_____

Product Reviews

☆☆☆☆☆

Product Name: _____

Company: _____

Thoughts:_____

_____

_____

_____

☆☆☆☆☆

Product Name: _____

Company: _____

Thoughts:_____

_____

_____

_____

☆☆☆☆☆

Product Name: _____

Company: _____

Thoughts:_____

_____

_____

_____

☆☆☆☆☆

Product Name: _____

Company: _____

Thoughts:_____

_____

_____

_____

Index

EXAMPLE

Category: _Finance_

Pages 4, 16, 54, 60

Category: _____

Pages _____

Category: _____

Pages _____

Category: _____

Pages _____

Category: _____

Pages _____

Category: _____

Pages _____

Category: _____

Pages _____

Category:_____

Pages _____

_____

_____

_____

Category:_____

Pages _____

_____

_____

_____

Category:_____

Pages _____

_____

_____

_____

Category:_____

Pages _____

_____

_____

_____

Category:_____

Pages _____

_____

_____

_____

Category:_____

Pages _____

_____

_____

_____

Category:_____

Pages _____

_____

_____

_____

ABOUT THE AUTHOR

Who is Kaylee?
Kaylee always wanted to be a writer when she grew up, and now a lifelong dream has come true. She is a self-published author and published her first book in 2016. The title is "New Baby, New You" It's a book about resolutions to help the new mom.

Kaylee has been keeping a journal and writing in a diary since the first grade. She enjoys writing short stories and now, writing on self-help topics which is another one of her passions. She's always trying to learn and grow and wants to help others do the same.

She was home-schooled, along with her brother, which allowed her the freedom to start her small handmade invitation business, Kards by Kaylee, when she was just 17 years old.

She is married to her high school sweetheart, and they have started a family together. She is the mother of a fiery little redhead. She is thankful for a hardworking husband who provides for their family so that she can continue to work from home.

Having always been goal-oriented, entrepreneurial, and continuously reading self-help books, she is a wealth of knowledge. Her goal is to inspire people with her words.

You can find her blog at www.kayleeberry.com and follow along with her latest writing projects.

"I'm excited to grow my following and help other bloggers along the way." –Kaylee

Writing Habit Creation Online Training Course

Take Control of Your Future and Get the Tools You Need to Achieve Your Dreams… And Increase Your Writing Productivity.

Are you like I was…struggling to find time to write and balancing family life. Do you have so many ideas for books or blog posts you're about to burst if you don't get them out? Are you looking to earn income writing part-time but are finding it hard to fit everything in a day? Do you want to write full time but lack the productivity you need to get everything done?

In this NEW Training, you will discover...

- Your "Why" for wanting to write so you can overcome any obstacle
- How to fit writing into your busy schedule
- Even spare moments can fuel your habit
- How to double or even triple your daily word count
- That you can build a daily habit that will stick
- How to always have inspiration
- The best way to reward your self and fuel your new habit
- How to reach your writing goals
- My 4-Step process to create any habit plus the tools to help you along the way
- And More!

Your message—your story–matters. Somebody is out there waiting for it. But if you don't have time to get your message out there into the world, it's not doing anybody and good… least of all you and your bank account.

Start creating the habit of writing everyday now!

http://kayleeberry.com/i-resolve-to-write/

TITLES IN THE SERIES "THE BLOG THAT NEVER ENDS"

Available Now

Fitness
Blog Planner
Journal

Coming Soon

Christian
Blog Planner
Journal

Craft
Blog Planner
Journal

Photography
Blog Planner
Journal

Made in the USA
Las Vegas, NV
25 August 2021